*Shame is the silent but deadly spirit, that lies dormant behind a false covering designed to keep you muzzled, bound, and chained to the pain of your past. This demonic principality has strategically been at work tangling you in Satan's web through disobedience, with the intent to use what was once your pride, to become the face of your shame. After the Altar!*

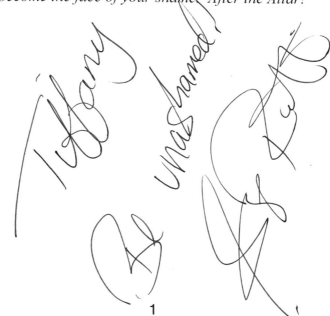

1

## *TABLE of CONTENTS*

**Chapter 1 – Shame**

**Chapter 2 – God is looking for you**

**Chapter 3 – Side effects of Shame**

**Chapter 4 – Functional Shame**

**Chapter 5 – You can be Free**

**Chapter 6 – How I overcame shame after sharing my story**

**Chapter 7 - Instead of Shame Double Honor**

Acknowledgements:


I would like to take this opportunity to thank my friend the Holy Spirit for downloading wisdom, and rare insight to complete this book, and for never leaving or forsaking me.

Thank you to my parents Doris Hodo, and Lindsey Ruffin. My siblings Alison Hodo Green, and Lindsey Ruffin Jr. To my beautiful grandmother Annie Mae Hodo, and host of family, and friends. I would like to show appreciation to my best friend Devon Mays, Kristy Rector, and my amazing god daughters. Thank you godmomma Lakenia Robinson for your on-going support. Each of your love, support, wisdom, and prayers played a key role in my life.

To all the leaders, mentors, and midwives, GOD has allowed to assist in imparting into my life, you are appreciated. Your intercession, and impartation made an impact in my life.

Special thanks to Amber McAfee-Barnes for the graphics, and sowing your gift into my life.

# Chapter One

## Shame

Shame is a silent but deadly spirit that begins its dirty work the moment of disobedience. Disobedience is the green apple you eat, and shame is the stomach ache that follows. You can't disobey, without suffering the aftermath, the backlash of shame manifesting. Where there is disobedience, and rebellion, there is shame awaiting, lingering, dripping with a blood thirsty desire to invade your life, and take up a permanent residence. Shame doesn't ask permission to gain entrance, shame is permitted, and granted access with an open door the moment you disobey the will of GOD. Shame has a role, and is strategic, so the demonic power works to push you into disobedience, to open the door for shame to walk in and take a seat on the throne of your heart. Shame is a principality, that refuses to leave even when you bind, rebuke, command it to come up, and come out. This principality is stubborn, and feels it has legal authority to reside in your temple. We will discuss later in the book on how to dismantle the strongman of Shame that has set up a demonic kingdom right under your nose. Shame will allow you to flow, shout, worship, and do all religious functions; however you're limited in space, capacity, realms, and dimensions. You can only go so far before shame, pulls you like a dog on a leash, commanding you to get back in your proper place. Shame is a demonic glory blocking spirit, and you must be set free before you can be all the GOD has ordained you to be.

Let's look at this deadly spirit, and how shame is connected to disobedience.

GENESIS 3: Now the serpent was more crafty than any of the wild animals the LORD God had made. He said to the woman, "Did God really say, 'You must not eat from any tree in the garden'?"

[2] The woman said to the serpent, "We may eat fruit from the trees in the garden, [3] but God did say, 'You must not eat fruit from the tree that is in the middle of the garden, and you must not touch it, or you will die.'"

[4] "You will not certainly die," the serpent said to the woman. [5] "For God knows that when you eat from it your eyes will be opened, and you will be like God, knowing good and evil."

[6] When the woman saw that the fruit of the tree was good for food and pleasing to the eye, and also desirable for gaining wisdom, she took some and ate it. She also gave some to her husband, who was with her, and he ate it

As I read this scripture, and study the role of Eve, and the serpent, I'm intrigued with how the enemy's strategy was to get Eve to "disobey" GOD. The serpent was crafty, skilled, and trained on how to strategically plant seed in the woman's mind to get her to lust, crave, desire something that she was instructed not to have. The enemy understands the downfall of disobedience, just look at where disobedience and an un-submitted spirit got him. CAST OUT. So the strategy was for the woman to defy GOD; which would open the door to shame. The enemy isn't invested in you tasting, becoming addicted, or getting involved in a situation. He's banking on you disobeying, so he can set up a demonic kingdom through shame with the intent to shut you down.

Disobedience is connected to things you want, things you desire, and things you crave; however the very thing you eat, can be the very thing that kills you. This act of disobedience was deadly, and caused the entire human race to suffer the consequences. The enemy comes after those who are chosen, pre-ordained, and destined to impact multiple lives, because if he can kill you, it will affect everyone assigned to your life. Just pause, and think about times you disobeyed GOD, and how your disobedience affected more than just you. Some of you are still paying the penalty, because shame has now muzzled your ministry. You are too ashamed to open your mouth and expose some of the places you've been. One of the enemies tactics is to use lust to lure you.

Lured by Lust:

Lust is more than sex, more than desiring to jump in the bedchamber with lovers. You can lust money; fame; ministry; platforms; relationships; material things, or as Eve she lusted the very idea that she would be like GOD. The enemy chatted with Eve long enough to gather information, to get inside of her head to begin the manipulation process. Eve revealed to the serpent what GOD permitted, and not permitted for them to have. She revealed the penalty of disobeying GOD would lead to death, and the enemy played her until she succumbed to his plan. The more the enemy spoke in her ear, the more desirable disobedience appeared. Disobedience has an appetite, and no matter how much you binge on disobedience you're never full, never satisfied. Disobedience is like chasing an addiction, that never satisfies or quenches the thirst. Disobedience and eating the wrong things will open your eyes to see more than you're built to handle.

The enemy desires to put you in situations where you will lust for the things GOD declares you can't have.

LUST is dangerous, it's a spermatic seed released, that leads to SIN, and the more you nurture that sin, you will give birth to a full blown LIFESTYLE; which is designed to kill you. The method of the enemy is to steal, kill, and destroy your destiny, and it begins with disobedience, lusting for something you were instructed not to Touch.

Your eyes open:

Genesis 3:7

Then the eyes of both of them were opened, and they realized they were naked; so they sewed fig leaves together and made coverings for themselves.

Once the eyes of Adam and Eve were opened, the very first manifestation of the enemy revealed was the Spirit of SHAME. They recognized their nakedness, and attempted to cover themselves with fig leaves. Shame immediately resulted in them seeking a false covering for shelter to hide the shame that was revealed. Shame will have you hustling around looking for a covering, to hid behind what you've done. The disobedience that happened Before Christ or After Christ will result in the same scenario, so this is what we have in common rather a non-believer or believer. When our eyes are open, and we are ashamed, we will seek a covering to hide behind our behavior. The enemy doesn't always seek to expose your nakedness, he desires for shame to lie dormant because you're just as ineffective. There are some things GOD wants to protect you from, there are things you don't need to see, so GOD put boundaries in place for protection.

The very things we done in our past, or even our future have led us to this same location, and that's to a destination called SHAME. Shame is that painful feeling of humiliation or distress caused by the consciousness of wrong or foolish behavior. You're humiliated, embarrassed, mortified, and feel a sense of guilt, regret, or sadness. Our behaviors, and acts of disobedience brings about shame especially for those who come to Christ. I want to address the shame that happens post altar. For those of you who know GOD, walk with GOD, serve GOD, and have a relationship with GOD. The shame that comes after the altar.

There were times in our walk where we were proud of our lifestyles. We were living that lifestyle with no convictions, and unashamed. Although, I'm using my personal story to share, I want you to put yourself in this situation, and use your scenario to track with me.

## **Snippet of my Story:**

During my time of living a homosexual lifestyle, I was proud of it. I was having a great time, enjoying my life, and doing everything I could to create the culture of being a part of the homosexual community. I was getting tattoos, drinking, smoking, involved with multiple women, and transforming my identity into a masculine stud where womanhood was completely foreign to me. I knew GOD's word regarding homosexuality; however I disobeyed GOD and quoted statements such as "this my life, and you only live once." I was so proud of being gay, I literally carried a chip on my shoulder. I would wear short sleeve shirts, and shorts to show off my tattoos, that I maintained, and kept oiled down, so they would be visible. I was out the closet, and everyone who knew me, knew I was gay. It's was no secret, I was bold and open about my lifestyle. I was a recruiter, and agent for the power of darkness, seeking to transform lives for the kingdom of darkness.

Then one Sunday, unintentionally, and unplanned I decided to attend a church service. This service ultimately changed my life forever. I was apprehended by the power of GOD, and found myself at the altar receiving prayer, deliverance, and break through. The power of GOD completely invaded my life, and transformed my life from darkness to light. I was born again, and sold out for the kingdom. My eyes were exposed to glory, to holiness, to righteousness, and from that moment on, I was converted to the kingdom of GOD. AS I walked through deliverance, I can recall shame invading my courts like a whirlwind. I was ashamed of what I was delivered from. The very thing that made me proud, turned around and humiliated me. I was ashamed of my identity, I was ashamed of my tattoos, I was ashamed to talk to friends, wondering if they would think I wanted them because of my past. I was tormented, and traumatized by the very thing that I boasted in. Who would of ever thought that the very thing I celebrated would turn around and torment me. Well I'm glad you asked. This was the enemy's strategy, and he had a plan to use shame to produce a counterfeit life after Christ. The enemy wanted me to hide, and find fig leaves to cover my shame.

*Can I be honest. Of course I can, it's me writing.*

I can recall my first relationship with a male after walking through deliverance. GOD had given me my beauty for ashes, and I was delivered from the residue of sin. I was rediscovering womanhood, and becoming comfortable in my identity. At this time a nice, attractive young man enters my life, and immediately before the relationship could be clearly established the enemy had set up plots in my mind by saying " you should have sex with him to prove you're delivered; you should get pregnant by him because if you have a baby no one will accuse you of being gay again; you should hurry up and attempt to get married." These tormenting words haunted me, and before I knew it, I was responding, and coming into agreement with these words.  During this time I was saved, sold out, and on fire for GOD .  I was teaching youth ministry, Sunday school, and active in church,.  The enemy doesn't care about your gift, or your anointing, if shame has you bound, he still has access.  As the words of the enemy lingered, I can recall dating this young man briefly before I found myself trying to get into his bedroom.  I didn't care about the sex, nor did I care much about him, but I needed his masculinity, and possibly his seed, so my shame could be covered.


I needed his presence as the fig leaves, to block the accusations, and shame that followed me post altar.  I didn't care about the consequences that followed, I needed my shame covered, and if it meant creating a counterfeit life, I was willing.

Then the LORD declared in a still small voice, I delivered you, I didn't set you back. He stated that if I created this counterfeit life out of shame, it would war with my future. The Scripture that came to mind was the story of Abram and Sarai. In Genesis 16 GOD began sharing how Sarai's shame of bareness, caused her to have her husband sleep with Hagar; which is the reason we are still at war. Ishmael's birth was out shame, and he's known as the counterfeit seed, who is waring with Isaac the promise. After this revelation, the Lord delivered me from the situation, and I began to walk through a journey of health, and wholeness.

Do you see how my life could have shifted in a matter of a decision. How shame was working strategically to get me to create a false life, and a false world. Here are a few examples of fig leave lives. There are many homosexuals who have married out of shame, and their life is now fig leaves. There are women reading this book who have married because you were pregnant, and didn't want to be a single mother so you married, and bound yourself with a man you don't even love. Some of you have become Pastor's out of shame deriving from church hurt, now you're pastoring a church with 10 members, when you're supposed to be preaching all over the world. Your fig leaves have become your covenant, and it's a false covenant if it was birth out of shame.

Shame isn't just after your life now, it works to build a counterfeit future.

What are your fig leaves, what have you used to cover your shame?

## Chapter 2

## GOD is looking for you

*Genesis 3:8-11*

*⁸ Then the man and his wife heard the sound of the LORD God as he was walking in the garden in the cool of the day, and they hid from the LORD God among the trees of the garden. ⁹ But the LORD God called to the man, "Where are you?"*

*¹⁰ He answered, "I heard you in the garden, and I was afraid because I was naked; so I hid."*

*¹¹ And he said, "Who told you that you were naked? Have you eaten from the tree that I commanded you not to eat from?"*

Shame will have you hide from man, and GOD. Many can hide, and get away with fig leaves when dealing with man, but who can hide from GOD. Who can hide from the GOD who is all knowing; all powerful; eyes in front, on the side, and behind Him. No one can hide from the

Creator of everything that is, was and is to come. In the midst of Adam & Eve using fig leaves to cover themselves, that covering couldn't hide them from the presence. GOD will come looking for you in the cool of the day. Shame keeps you from the presence of the LORD, and will have you breaking your normal flow, and routine. Even while hiding, GOD called for them, and sought them out. GOD was well aware of their disobedience, but the Father still kept his end of the deal, and came looking for them.

GOD is looking for many of you who are hiding. Your shame has pushed you out of the presence of the LORD. GOD is seeking you, HE's released an amber alert in the spirit realm, attempting to locate you. Some of you are hiding behind tongues, prophecies, microphones, and platforms, using your gift as a fig leave to hide your shame. God is seeking those who are bound by shame, and under a false covering. Shame is that very thing that you are sensitive about, you don't want it touched, you reject any form of prophesy or word in that area, because you're too ashamed, and the fear of being disappointed again is unbearable. We have some of the greatest leaders who can't go to the next level, because the very thing they are called to speak about, they are muzzled by shame. Some marriages that survived infidelity needs to be ministered, but you to ashamed, so you keep silent. You've had abortions, but you have vowed yourself not to ever preach about that, because of the shame. You've dealt with barrenness, but you won't speak on it because the shame it carriers. You've been delivered from masturbation; pornography; rape; molestation, and incest, but again you won't share it because of the shame. Some of you are allowing other's to tell their stories, all while you continue to preach a counterfeit message, due to your shame muzzling your mouth and dictating what you can and can't say. GOD is looking for you. Your shame has gone undetected long enough, and it's keeping you from the presence of the LORD.

GOD is looking to restore you, and ask you WHO told you, you were naked. GOD wants to deal with the shame in your life, and cover you, so you can move into the realm of ministry you're called into. When GOD comes to look for you, it's to discipline you, deal with your enemy, and restore you by clothing you with the proper garments. When GOD came looking for Adam, and Eve, GOD handed out the consequences; however GOD covered them. GOD wants to cover you. It's time to remove the fig leaves, and get covered properly.

Shame is a destiny blocking spirit. The enemy doesn't want you to experience proper covering, so he will keep you distracted by your false garments . Some has functioned so long with fig leaves, you believe that's the life you were destined to have. Shame will allow you to go forth, but you're not effective to the capacity GOD has called you to. GOD is so good HE will discipline you, then cover you.

# Chapter 3

## Side Effects of Shame

Have you ever taken medication, and read the back before taking that prescription? The first thing I assess before taking any medication is the side effects. Side effects reveal to you a list of things that may occur, and states if you experience these side effects throw away the prescription, or see a doctor. I believe if you are aware of the side effects of shame, you will CAST it OUT, and if that doesn't work, you will see the Physician. Jesus is the Physician you need to contact regarding this principality. God wants to set you free. Shame is a stubborn power, it's too ashamed to admit it's shame; therefore, shame remains legal, and continues to reside inside of you. I come to shine light on shame, and let you know that your anointing can no longer be your filter. We live in the age of the filter, and many saints have used their theology; wisdom; gift, and call as a filter to hide the shame. I prophesy that the filter loses its power, and you come into agreement with your deliverance as you read this book.

## Counterfeit:

As mentioned in the previous chapter, shame produces a counterfeit life. Shame drives you into the arms of lovers; addictions; and idolatry. Shame will prophesy, and create a life based on the conditions of your situation. You will marry prematurely; have children prematurely; invest in materialistic items to cover up etc. Many of you are unhappy, and asking how did you end up in the situations you are in, how did you marry who you married, how did you choose the career path you've chosen. Some of you have chosen your career based on your childhood experiences of poverty, so you do something you hate to get you out the hood, but you're not in purpose, and still unhappy. This enemy is demonic and will allow you to live, just not the life you were preordained to live for the kingdom. People die with shame, and their entire adult life in the earth was a counterfeit.

## Paranoia:

Shame produces paranoia. You're constantly worried about what people are saying about you, who's looking at you etc. You spend more time focusing on the opinion of others, and this hinders you from healthy appropriate relationships. You have delusions of being persecuted, unwarranted jealous, or exaggerated self-importance. You're very suspicious, and often give people the side eye, anticipating an attack. You have a strong mistrust for people without evidence or justification. You're anxious, and often feel it's a conspiracy against you.

## Anxiety:

Shame produces anxiety. You have distress, and it hinders you from carrying out day to day life. You get anxious when people touch on the situation you're shameful about, and begin to show signs of nervousness, discomfort, and irritability. You feel a sense of turmoil, uneasy, and worry.

## Fear:

Shame produces fear. Fear of being judged, fear of someone finding out your secret. A sense of terror, alarm, and panic makes you dread certain conversation, people and places.

## False Security:

Shame produces false security. Your fig leaves have become your covering. You feel that you are safe, and everything is alright because you're able to function. You are covered well, and the counterfeit life you have is secured tightly. There is no concern of your cover being revealed.

## Bitter Soul:

Shame produces a bitter soul. You've been so disappointed by GOD, you are numb and bitter. You've walked with shame for so long, your mentality has become "it is what it is." You're content with the outcome of your life, and have settled with the bitter soul, believing the lies of the enemy that GOD failed you.  You are functioning with a bitter soul.

**Muzzles you:**

Shame will muzzle your mouth, giving you the right to remain silent because you don't want anyone to know your secret.  Your ministry is ineffective in that particular area, because although GOD has delivered you, you won't be the blueprint for someone else.  You're silenced, and your lips are sealed.  No matter how much GOD press you to speak because someone needs your testimony, you will take the secret to the grave.

**Poor Posture:**

Shame will have you hang your head low, slack your posture and hunch  your back.  Your body language and countenance is dimmed, and altered.

**Pride:**

Shame produces pride. Shame will have you un-submitted in areas GOD wants you to yield. Shame takes the focus off the deliverer, and points the finger towards you. You become worried about how it will make you look, what people will say about you, how you feel about it, and it becomes all about you.

There are other side effects to shame, but these are some of the side effects I personally endured through my journey of deliverance.

# Chapter 4

## Functional Shame

Have you ever heard of functional addicts? A functioning addict is someone who is able to hid the excesses of their alcohol or drug use. An example of a functioning alcoholic is on who have a good job, a secure home life, and respected in the community despite drinking an excessive amount of alcohol . This person has the strength, balance, and tenacity to handle both lifestyles very well. They tend to support their children, pay bills on time, love on their spouses, and perform well at work. If you was to see that alcoholic in an environment where he's not drinking, you may not pick up on their private addiction. They have mastered the craft of balancing a normal life outside of their addiction.

People who have skilled themselves on balancing multiple worlds without lacking in area are dangerous. They are able to live a life, while low-key entertaining a secret side. The enemy has released this spirit in the church. We have functioning shame going on in the house of GOD. Some of you have mastered the craft of being a Christian, while bound with shame. You are able to maintain a position in the church; pay your tithes, and prophesy accurately, while underneath you're full of shame. No one is able to detect it because it's draped in the coverings of religion. The enemy is allowing you to go forth, with a leash on, that is a constant reminder of how far you can go.

You can walk with shame for so long, you forget it's with you, until something happens and you're reminded that it's still there. Some of you desire to write a book, and share your story, but you can't because you still too ashamed to reveal the secret of the uncle molesting all of the children. Shame will lie dormant, until the enemy comes to attack someone you love with the very same thing you're ashamed to reveal.

Those who deal with functional shame has the ability to go unrecognized for years. They work overtime to keep up their appearance to prevent from being detected. They can hold down a position in the church, maintain a filtered like on social media, all while hiding their demons from the ones they love most. Functioning shame is so good at masking, and covering up, they are unable to receive assistance until it's too late. The enemy has already moved in and created the counterfeit life.

Functioning shame makes excuses for their behavior. When shame is addressed, the enemy will have you put up a wall of defense, by creating excuses to hide from being revealed. Shame will justify itself, and you will find yourself defending the spirit, that needs to be CAST OUT. You will cover your shame, and will Shamar (govern, and protect) the very enemy that's destroying your life. You're loyal to this spirit, you've invested in your fig leaves, and now the spirit of pride stands at the gate shielding off any who would attempt to confront the shame in your life. This level of shame feeds off the rewards of going undetected, and will tell you that if you let go of shame you will suffer significant loss.

Functioning shame will do more than what it's intended to do. This enemy will have your life spiral out of control by simply keeping you in a state of hiding. The enemy will create a life for you on the side, and will convince you that this is the ordained will of GOD for your life. Just imagine if I would have listened to shame. I would have created a world that was not the will of GOD. That world would have been birth out of shame, and my life would be different from what it is now. Shame attempted to go beyond the realm of embarrassment. Shame has the ability to pro-create and bring into existence with the attempt to war with your destiny. I would have brought in a child, a relationship, and my lineage would have derived from shame. Let's take a look at this deeper.

When you allow shame to procreate, it doesn't present to you things that don't appear real. This enemy presents a real life, with real characters, and the people you bring into your world out of shame, have no clue that they are counterfeits. Some of you reading this book, know that you married the person to cover your shame. Some of you minsters who are single, were pressured to marry, so instead of being ashamed, you married someone and they have become your fig leaves. The enemy doesn't play fair, so even in marrying someone out of shame, the enemy will give you a false peace and happiness. It's not a matter of you marrying the wrong person and being miserable, the assignment is to abort the original purpose in which you were sent into the earth.

Shame is a birthing spirit, a reproducing spirt that has the power to bring a life into existence. The enemy's strategy is to keep you from the perfect will of GOD, even if he has to create a false life to abort your purpose.

## Chapter 5

## You can be free

I can recall times I was functioning with shame. Shame doesn't like to be exposed, because once exposed you're free. The way to defeat shame is to tell on it. When you have lived to tell it, you have access to destroy that principality and tear down its kingdom. GOD doesn't want you to function in shame, GOD wants you to destroy it. Shame has no power when it's told on. The enemy operates against us using blackmail, and making threats to expose us; however, when you tell on yourself, hell loses its power. The strength of the enemy is the secrets you are ashamed of. There are things you've gotten yourself in, and the first thing we do is look for ways to hide it, and cover it. You have the power in you to destroy Satan, and the web he has built to destroy, and alter your destiny. Shame will allow you to be delivered from addictions, habits, and craves, all while going untouched. The moment you receive deliverance, the shame that lies dormant, opens the door, and invites them spirits back home.

You were delivered to become the deliverer for someone else. You have the power to be free from Shame, and produce a Samuel.

I'm reminded of Hannah, and how she responded to shame. 1 Samuel 1: Hannah a barren woman, shamed by her barrenness, and inability to get pregnant by her husband. Hannah was tormented by her husband's other wife a Peninnah's ability to have children. Instead of Hannah covering, and hiding her shame, she responded with vulnerability; transparency; and humility. Hannah went and sought the LORD with everything in her. She was open for visitation, and GOD responded. Sometimes you are so ashamed you don't have words, but the proper approach to GOD will bend HIS ear towards your heart, and your request will be made known. Hannah cried out, and her tears articulated a language until the heavens responded. The proper approach to shame can bless you beyond measure. Hannah demonstrates the perfect example of how to deal with shame.

*1* *1-2* *There once was a man who lived in Ramathaim. He was descended from the old Zuph family in the Ephraim hills. His name was Elkanah. (He was connected with the Zuphs from Ephraim through his father Jeroham, his grandfather Elihu, and his great-grandfather Tohu.) He had two wives. The first was Hannah; the second was Peninnah. Peninnah had children; Hannah did not.*

*3-7* *Every year this man went from his hometown up to Shiloh to worship and offer a sacrifice to GOD-of-the-Angel-Armies. Eli and his two sons, Hophni and Phinehas, served as the priests of GOD there. When Elkanah sacrificed, he passed helpings from the sacrificial meal around to his wife Peninnah and all her children, but he always gave an especially generous helping to Hannah because he loved her so much, and because GOD had not given her children. But her rival wife taunted her cruelly, rubbing it in and never letting her forget that GOD had not given her children. This went on year after year. Every time she went to the sanctuary of GOD she could expect to be taunted. Hannah was reduced to tears and had no appetite.*

*8* *Her husband Elkanah said, "Oh, Hannah, why are you crying? Why aren't you eating? And why are you so upset? Am I not of more worth to you than ten sons?"*

*9-11 So Hannah ate. Then she pulled herself together, slipped away quietly, and entered the sanctuary. The priest Eli was on duty at the entrance to GOD's Temple in the customary seat. Crushed in soul, Hannah prayed to GOD and cried and cried—inconsolably. Then she made a vow: Oh, GOD-of-the-Angel-Armies,*
*If you'll take a good, hard look at my pain,*
*If you'll quit neglecting me and go into action for me*
*By giving me a son,*
*I'll give him completely, unreservedly to you.*
*I'll set him apart for a life of holy discipline.*

*12-14 It so happened that as she continued in prayer before GOD, Eli was watching her closely. Hannah was praying in her heart, silently. Her lips moved, but no sound was heard. Eli jumped to the conclusion that she was drunk. He approached her and said, "You're drunk! How long do you plan to keep this up? Sober up, woman!"*

*15-16 Hannah said, "Oh no, sir—please! I'm a woman hard used. I haven't been drinking. Not a drop of wine or beer. The only thing I've been pouring out is my heart, pouring it out to GOD.*

*Don't for a minute think I'm a bad woman. It's because I'm so desperately unhappy and in such pain that I've stayed here so long."*

*[17] Eli answered her, "Go in peace. And may the God of Israel give you what you have asked of him."*

*[18] "Think well of me—and pray for me!" she said, and went her way. Then she ate heartily, her face radiant.*

*[19] Up before dawn, they worshiped GOD and returned home to Ramah. Elkanah slept with Hannah his wife, and GOD began making the necessary arrangements in response to what she had asked.*

### Dedicating the Child to God

*[20] Before the year was out, Hannah had conceived and given birth to a son. She named him Samuel, explaining, "I asked GOD for him."*

## Chapter Six

### *How I overcame Shame after telling my testimony*

Many of you know my story of deliverance from the spirit of homosexuality. If you don't please read my books "From Point Guard to Prophet" and "After the Altar." These books share my story of deliverance from the lifestyle of homosexuality that had me bound for years. However; I want to expose a spirit that I struggled with after sharing my testimony, and telling on the enemy. Revelations 12:11 Declares they overcame him by the blood of the Lamb, and by the word of their testimony, and they love their lives to the death. Yes, I overcame him by the word of my testimony; however the backlash of shame experienced was unbearable, and tormenting. I was in functioning in ministry, active, loving GOD, and sharing my story, all while shame was trying to manifest, and get the best of me. February 2016, I took a bold leap, and unplanned, and unintentionally shared my personal story in great detail on periscope. The Holy Spirit arrested my lips, and before I knew it, I was blasting my business, and exposing to the world my personal story.

Instantly the story was traveling at a rapid speed, as many were becoming familiar with my story, and labeling me, "the woman who was delivered from homosexuality." The doors began opening, at a momentum that knocked me off my feet. I began to travel nearly every weekend, sharing the good news, and testifying how GOD delivered and set me free. GOD would have me look back over my life, and how HE brought me out of the pit, and I would compare before and after pictures, that shocked me. The pictures were going viral, my testimony was going viral, and boom immediately following an amazing service, shame knocked on the doors of my soul. Wait, hold up, not you again I responded to shame. Shame knocked harder, and I found myself looking for fig leaves to cover what I was feeling. I was now on a platform with many eyes looking, and shame decided to show up. Awkward how shame will use others to push you further into shame, by using a false word from the LORD to usher you into a false covering.

Immediately I started struggling with shame. Shame would say, "Everyone knows your story; why did you tell it; people don't believe you're delivered; they going to watch you closely when you talk to women; you better hurry and get married, you need some children." The shame talk tormented me so strong, I attempted to put head phones on to block the noise. When the shame became strong, I found myself prepared to entertain premature relationship with men to cover my shame. The enemy looks for Kairos moments to come back around to launch the same attack. After recognizing the enemy, and his strategy because I been down this road before, I responded immediately. I exposed it, and that's why I am writing this book, that's why I'm preaching this message, so you can be free. Once I exposed the enemy for who he was, I had the power to cast him out. I had the authority to deal with him, and demolish his demonic coalition that was being implemented. GOD gave me wisdom, and rare insight on dealing with this principality. I assessed the barriers of shame, I prioritized the strong man connected, and I gave the battle to GOD. I refused to go into hiding, I refused to get entangled in a false coverings. I brought the issue to GOD, and was transparent; which stripped the enemy of his power. GOD intervened, and instead of shame GOD promoted me, and gave me double honor. GOD reminded me that I was dead, I crucified my flesh, and my story wasn't about me, it was to bring glory and honor to the kingdom. GOD removed the muzzle that was trying to bind me from speaking. Even when others begged me to stop sharing my story, GOD revealed that their shame was speaking, and my boldness was an indictment against them.

People will attempt to muzzle you, and encourage you to be silent, when your boldness convicts them for being ashamed. The enemy is raising up an army of those who are will to be persecuted for the kingdom. Those who are willing to put their lives at stake for the glory of GOD being manifested. Your shame is keeping you from the being the voice of deliverance for the people you're ordained to reach. You've become numb to your shame, and my prayer is this book rattle you, and set you free. You have places to go, people to meet, and things to do. Hiding behind the 4 walls of the church is ineffective to the kingdom, you have stunted your growth, and shame has arrested your development. The enemy will have you investing time, energy, and concentration in an assignment you've outgrown. GOD is ready to use your story, use your life, and use your shame to be the blueprint for someone else.

There is a generation arising that are unchurched. These rookies are the replacement for many who have disobeyed the directives of the KING. The Esther's are arising who will have uncommon favor with the king. GOD is preparing you, stirring you, and equipping you to come forth, and be the voice of deliverance for bloodlines. The road of Damascus is being highlighted, and GOD is taking people off the streets, cleaning them up, and using them mightily. Many have prophesied the homosexuals are coming; the drug addicts are coming; the misfits are coming; the pedophiles are coming; the prostitutes are coming. You have seen well, and have prophesied accurately. For they are not coming, they have arrived, and the gates of hell shall not prevail against them.

They will be Comeback Kids, who will go back and get those who are bound by the very spirit, they were delivered from.

Don't miss this move of GOD. Get delivered from your shame. It doesn't matter if you're 50, 60, or 70, if you have breath in your body, you can deal with the shame. You may have grandchildren who needs your story, .so they don't repeat the same cycle you made. GOD wants to deliver you from shame, and release a supernatural blessing of double honor upon you.

Shame has lost its grip. The only covering I have is the Blood of Jesus, that has set me free. Whom the SON sets free, is free indeed.

# Chapter Seven

## Instead of shame Double Honor

*Isaiah 61:7 Instead of your shame
you will receive a double portion,
and instead of disgrace
you will rejoice in your inheritance.
And so you will inherit a double portion in your
land,
and everlasting joy will be yours.*

The Lord has made a promise to give you double honor instead of shame. Shame has the ability to be replaced. GOD is aware that you will encounter shame, so HE promise to upgrade your life with double honor. Not just honor but double honor. With honor comes favor; promotion; wealth; blessings; and influence. When people question the honor that's on your life, advise them that shame promoted you. Shame will promote you when you yield it to GOD to be set free. You will never experience the realm of double honor, if you're walking with shame.  GOD is declaring that instead of disgrace, you will rejoice in your inheritance. You're in a position of inheritance, and you will inherit a double portion in your land, and everlasting joy.

I prophesy that this book has stirred you, and charged you to tell it.  Exposing the spirit of shame will unlock double honor, double favor; double promotion; double glory, and double portion upon your life.  You've wondered why you've been functioning in ministry, but haven't experienced the good of the LORD in the land of the living.  It's the shame that has tangled you, and allowed you to function.  You've been a puppet for the powers of darkness right in the house of God.  Today renounce shame.  Expose it for what it is, and receive your blessing.  I declare that the muzzle is being removed from your mouth, and declare that you will speak boldly and unhindered.  I prophesy that the power of GOD will cause you to remove the fig leaves, and cover you HIMSELF.

Made in the USA
Middletown, DE
05 July 2017